The Abundance of Nothing

Also by Bruce Weigl

The Abundance
of Nothing

Poems

Bruce Weigl

TRIQUARTERLY BOOKS

NORTHWESTERN UNIVERSITY PRESS

EVANSTON, ILLINOIS

TriQuarterly Books
Northwestern University Press
www.nupress.northwestern.edu

Printed in the United States of America

10   9   8   7   6   5   4   3   2

Library of Congress Cataloging-in-Publication Data
Weigl, Bruce, 1949–
    The abundance of nothing : poems / Bruce Weigl.
       p. cm.
    ISBN 978-0-8101-5223-6 (pbk. : alk. paper)
    I. Title.
  PS3573.E3835A64 2012
  811.54—dc23

                                                          2011036086

♾ The paper used in this publication meets the minimum requirements of the American
National Standard for Information Sciences—Permanence of Paper for Printed Library
Materials, ANSI Z39.48-1992.

For Pham Tien Duat,
in memoriam

as all the many sides of life
whiz by,
a blast at best, a loss

Robert Creeley
(in homage)

Contents

Part II: My Waiting Brain

Part III: Meditation After Prayer

Acknowledgments

I offer my grateful acknowledgment for the support of the editors of magazines in which versions of these poems first appeared. I also offer my enduring gratitude for the Lannan Foundation and staff, and the Lannan family, for their belief in my work and for their generous support of my writing life. Additional thanks are due to Andrew Weigl for his close reading of some of these poems and to Chase Twitchell for her good ear and eye. Without the help of my daughter and her intimate understanding of her culture, many of these poems could not have been written. My gratitude to Reg Gibbons for his always generous editorial help and advice is offered here, and last, I am grateful to Nguyen Ba Chung for his lessons in the dharma, and to Kevin Bowen for taking me to see the monk on the mountain in Hue. I want also to acknowledge the work of my friend and colleague, the poet Nguyen Phan Que Mai, for her work on some of these poems.

American Poetry Review: "The Abundance of Nothing," "Bill," "I Almost Didn't See," "One Lie," "On the Little Juniata River," "Paradise of Pain," "Roses for the Reader," "This Boy," "When I'm Gone," and "The World, Part I"

Blackbird: "For Penelope," "Response to 'Why Don't You Write About Something Happy?,'" and "Pastoral as Complaint"

Chariton Review: "Beginning," "Conundrum," "Ice Storm," "Self-Portrait After 'Hotel Insomnia,'" and "Wrong"

Columbia Poetry Review: "Meditation After Prayer"

Consequence: "Apocryphal Weather," "The Father in Me," and "Letter to L."

Field: "The Deer Cave Drawing in Southern China That the Chinese Girl Drew on the Napkin to Show Me Exactly Where the Character Now Used for the Word Deer Came From" and "Elegy for Liam"

Flights: "My Checkered Past"

Folio: "The Way Dante Moved Virgil Through Hell"

Great River Review: "My Dimension"

Kenyon Review: "The Country That We Love" and "My Waiting Brain"

New Ohio Review: "Reunion"

New Republic: "She Said, 'But It Was Only a Small Hurt' "

New York Quarterly: "The Caves at Bai Non Nuoc" (as "The Caves China Beach") and "The End of My Career in Dance"

New York Times: "In the Rest of the World, the Worry Is Very Big"

Normal School: "Conundrum," "Meditation After Prayer," "To No Spirits Speak," and "What Are You Going to Do"

Paris Review: "For My Neighbors"

Poet Lore: "South Lorain Suite"

Prairie Schooner: "Elegy for the Dead, Whom I Love," "Flash," "The Future," "The Quiet Fountain," and "The Room"

Salmagundi: "A Little Place on the Beach"

Solo: "Thank You for Thinking of You"

TriQuarterly: "My Dimension" and "My Nymphomaniac"

The Abundance of Nothing

PART I

My Dimension

Quiet Fountain

I love the guest house on Nguyen Du. I slept

    inside the linen net, my windows open wide

        to let the spirits in who come to visit

from the lake. I've seen them in a chorus,

    their white shapes in the garden where the lotus blossom

        has to be content to swirl in

just one place, the fishpond crowded, the quiet fountain

    only barely there. I share my room

        with geckos on the wall who chirp their discontent—

the lack of bugs, my modern pesticides—

    and with a rat who visits when I shower;

        he cleans himself beside me on the floor,

    and soon, I wash like him, beyond the gaze

        that knows there's room for both of us to live.

The End of My Career in Dance

What I have in my head is a wail of words that sometimes makes sense if I can
      hold on to their wildness long enough
to tell you how the air around your face in the half-light Texas evening
      shone. The only way around the truth is to lie. *I am nothing*
without you, should be more difficult to say,
      or it must mean that there's some riff
in the flow of how things ought to be,
      some disruption that needs mending with a kiss,
followed by a thousand more kisses,
      and a light only eyes can share
across the distance named longing.
      There were witnesses to this,
including angels,
      so you don't have to take my word alone.
There's love, and then there's nothing, and it took my breath away
      like a hand around my throat, or like a pistol
pressed to my head, is how I remember it.

Conundrum

Late winter storm makes it all white again; late March and so cold I

can't get warm in my skin, and although I wanted to sing outside,

I pissed instead a circle into the snow because I could. I don't know
if this is a conundrum or not, but my brain is free of hardware
so the words come in a new order, like laps of waves to the needy shore, oh boy.

I married the wife of the sky, and I don't know if that means trouble or not,
but secrets course through her skin.
On the road inside her, her love wildly grows. No exits. That love.

My Checkered Past

A painted dog keeps coming to my head;
he's red and black, no bigger than your hand,
     as if he's painted on a piece of wood.
I don't know who the dog in question is;
     there are so many in my checkered past
including those that I betrayed sometimes
     to death. I left one in an angry field with an angry man
I knew would want to kill the dog for nothing more
     than nothing else to do.
He said he couldn't hunt; he might as well be dead.
     I took the easy way because I wasn't brave. I turned away,
I could not watch his face. A painted dog keeps coming to my head.

Thank You for Thinking of You

I stood in the dirty snow, the slag soot-stained snow
around the steel mill neighborhood
in a too-thin jacket
shivering for my shabby sins.
Thank you, nurse, who let my heart bleed out
one lonely post-neurological night.
I could swim or I could drown,
depending on your illegitimate care.
Thank you Sgt. X, for leaving me
behind on the abandoned LZ,
where all night small arms fire
crackled in the trees along the river,
night of my downfall that won't go away.
Thank you teacher, coach,
who fondled my dick and my balls,
telling me I had to be *checked*.
Now are the lost days
I calculate with the digits of your cold hands.
Thank you for thinking of you.

I Almost Didn't See

The toad was trapped; the drain was overflowed
from flooded downspouts in a summer storm.
       He was a young and handsome toad, still lean from tadpole days,
so I wanted to reach down
       to lift him from the whirlpool he struggled to survive, but I wavered there.

I'd come outside to watch the storm roll in its black and roiled clouds,
       the rain we needed, rare as peace.
He had to learn how not to die himself.
       He didn't drown; I didn't reach to pull him out.

In the Rest of the World, the Worry Is Very Big

As if this is the world
       you would make: nakedness,
captionless photographs,

grim motels drenched in night
       rain, love in foreign places,
like where the soldiers

cry, and hold your hand down
       Bernauer Strasse, by the small
lake on which you watched

the eclipse, holding the little
       girl's hand, and shading her
eyes, all those suffering

years ago, the memory
       of murder (themselves and
the others) hanging

in the air like a mist. Some of us
       think we're not dead,
only chagrined, all propaganda reduced,

like everything else,
       to metaphor.
Some people make up

reasons to kill you
       in your sleep, while you
face the door, wall at your

back (or like the day the
        old man butchered
the coop full of pigeons

because they kept flying
        back home). Anything murdered
makes a horrible cry.

Ice Storm

I got my own personal Jacob's ladder,
     buddy, reader, listener to this
          sad song. I built a temple for the ghosts
because they just kept coming. When I try
     to sing, I have a lark in my throat.
          I like it when the words are little
daggers, flying through the air like frozen rain.

My Dimension

Beautiful weather here now,
    if you're blind. Summer,
        with that fall bite in the night air,

    and through my window,
        the tree frogs hum like a flood.

        We don't like redundancies.

    We think only other people repeat their stories.

        I thought I saw a world.

    I thought I saw someone's

boot on someone else's neck.

Elegy for the Dead, Whom I Love

The cemetery walls in disrepair,

      some markers even toppled by the roving boys

who come at night to damage what they can,

      as if to leave some wreckage in their wake.

And it's not right to do this to the dead;

not even stupid idleness should lead them here.

      Yet they have come and gone; the day will soon

forget their names; the dead will bear it all

      and won't complain, their headstones knocked away.

Self-Portrait After "Hotel Insomnia"

i

I wanted my little planet,
      its heart eating the brick patio,
yet sparing the guests.
      Next door was a peacock.
A few cities ago,
      a crippled infant came to dine—
my blue baby.

ii

Mostly though, it was brilliant:
      each bosom with its spider of heavy jewelry,
bathing its ax in a tub
      of cigarette lies and insignificant loss.
So sweet,
      I could not ease my pain, even with the moving van.

iii

At 5 A.M., the twist of bare bodies
      everywhere, and the murderous nanny,
whose tunnel is in the ghetto,
      longs to vote after a campaign of lies.
Once too, the "eek" of a toy, breaking.
      So near it was, I surrendered
my body. I waited for the vision.

Johnny

I've walked all day through corn stubble fields of snow
hunting rabbits, and killed more than a few,
and later cooked and ate them too
with my friend who killed many rabbits beside me.
I loved him. We wrestled like brothers
in the summer grass and slept together
in a sleepover bed. Now he's alive
inside his dream of an airplane

crashing into mountains, his friends dead and bloody
in the wreckage, and he safe at home
in the West Virginia of his guilt. I grieve
for the frozen bodies in the snow.
I grieve for my friend who believes
he should have been with them no matter what you say.
I grieve for the rabbits I blasted
painfully into death; like me,
they were only souls,
being something in the world, ever after.

The Caves at Bai Non Nuoc

The children want to take me to the caves;
  they grab my hand and lead me in the dark.
    The story in the village says two soldiers,
who were lost and without guns, had wandered
  down the village road, perhaps to see
    what light it could have been that shined ahead—
the temple where the students wrote their prayers.
  The people's soldiers owned the night; they knew
    that they had visitors: the word passed all
along the beach and village road. A boy
  who's only four or five warns me to watch
    my head. Inside the cave it's cool. He shines
his light and says, *that's where they died. They tried*
  to hide inside the cave, he says, and laughs.

Bill

Someone had left him in the cold,
the black and white cat I found at the pound,
and the kind people took him in
once they had reported to work.
They put him in a cage with a blanket, some food and water,
where I found him,
and how could I have said no to Bill,
named to honor my uncle
who'd won a Silver Star
for glider landings in the dark, and who asked the nurse,
the last time I took him to the VA hospital, in Lorain, Ohio,
which is another kind of story, just days before he died,
"You don't work for that Kevorkian, do you?"
Bill lies across the table where I try to work. He stretches his long body
precisely out across the paper
so it's impossible to write a single word.

The Room

I didn't want to ever lose your face,
    the way you found me in the darkened room,
        my brain an open wound and me not sure
of anything. The gurney wheels brought me
    here to you; the morphine freely came,
        yet it was more the sweetness of your voice,
the way your hand felt on my brow, the way
    you leaned the weight of you against the pull
        of other duties waiting down the hall
that eased me back, the anesthesia gone.
    Then I awoke, and you no longer there,
        and what I wanted has the name of everything:
the brain relieved, the pretty scar, the room
    whose dark I lavished in, and you in me.

My Life with Cats

Cats are easily inhabited by the dead.
If you call a new cat by the name
of a recently dead,
the dead will come back inside of that cat.

I've seen this happen in my own family.

I've seen cats curl around cancer
not yet diagnosed, night after night.

Cats will prolong the kill
like no other animal
except humans.

Pastoral as Complaint

The robin is so quarrelsome. He barks
to no one in the trees; he fluffs his body
twice its size and rattles in the leaves.
He doesn't know or won't accept
the nest is empty now; the eggs are broken
on the ground. The storm was quick, we didn't
see it come; no sound above the hum
a summer morning makes when god is in
her place and we are free of tragedies
that pile up along the way. The robin
is so quarrelsome; he thinks his life
is gone just like the nest, but he is like
the rest of us, it's only now begun;
his life without her, only now begun.

My Mother, Fading

      The skunks tear up the yard for grubs,
but I will not wait up;
they are too many, and what could you do?

      Cold, but the sun out all day, and my mother
in her new forgetfulness
says over and over,

      how lovely it is that it's cold,
but that the sun is out too.
In her eyes for the first time,

      the terrified look the lost
almost imperceptibly assume,
mad beyond our maddening, irrelevant care.

      I take her by her hand, to show her
where the skunks had fed for grubs
and tore my lawn to shreds; she laughs.

One Lie

The light suffuses me, dearest ones,
you who expect me to live forever; the light
shoots straight through my body, although I can
grit my teeth now to almost any pain, and even

miss the pain when it's gone, as when the light is gone
at the boundary between things. That's all I want to say
about that now, because the howls and the cries of
all the people abandoned in the storm Katrina

are like the radical flaw of reason, like
the insufficiency of reason, as seen
in the bodies of people floating in the floodwaters
of the Mississippi. You can tie things together

if you like. You can say that one thing is connected
to the other, and so on, and so forth, on past our wildest
imaginings, so that you may believe that the world is
held together somehow, and that the shapes of things,

and the million dialogues, and the billion monologues
all add up to something discernible, sometimes something even holy.
Anyhow, it's a beautiful lie. It's a lie you can strap on
and live with for a long time, and imagine is your life.

My Nymphomaniac

Too young to know any god
damn thing about women I stood in the
alley with one Karen Mendez who
told me she was a nympho and who said she
had a rubber, neither of which I could
identify but I could tell from the
way her eyes lit up in the dark alley
and the way she moved her thirteen-year-old
body in the fractured light that came
to us there that something important
was about to happen then she reached her
long fingers under the legs of my shorts and
found me so my legs straightened out on their
own as if I were at attention then
she kissed my mouth so I couldn't breathe my
god and she pulled her own shorts off and tried
to climb up on top of me there in the
alley and I began to think that I'd
made a mistake and set myself up for
some trouble as the alley closed in on us
like night and she rubbed against me
in a rhythm I remembered from some other
time and place and I could hear voices from the
corner where my pals hung out whom I longed
for, and I could hear music from someone's
record player leak out into the night
sky and seem to settle there for a moment
and then disappear

For My Neighbors

The faux stone naked torsos in my neighbor's garden must signify something,
as this coffin I carry around on my back means something—
my bed, or my field to lay myself down in—you know. I love my neighbors,
even the ones I don't know, and so must imagine lives for; even those
who hide behind their curtains in the heavy odor of their secrets
that spread and tangle like vines until there is nothing left to see or to love.
We are all in this together, this lawn mowing and leaf raking until death,
this trash hauling and gutter cleaning metaphysics; it's what we have
in common, and I am grateful for the dogs walked past my house,
and for their shrill barking in the early morning cold, like today for example,
and even though you don't know my name, I am happy to be among you,
safe in our unspoken village, the walls of our courtesy
like broken glass–embedded stone.

Self-Portrait in the Third Person at Fifty-Eight

I knocked on the door of his forehead, but there was nobody home,
so I looked into his eyes and saw straight through to another time.
I shouted into his ear, but only whimpers came back, only cries,
because that's his nature, as it's the scorpion's

nature to sting the frog who lets it ride its back across the river
so they both drown. When he drowned, he later remembered it
as only a slightly uncomfortable moment or two of confusion,
because that's the way he's come to love the body's frail way,
the winding down to dust along the road, *bui doi.*

Reunion

As the *popular* girl walks among us with the microphone,
most of our stories are about loss,
or include exquisitely precise
medical and pharmaceutical details,
as if the words could suture the wounds, or save us even one last breath.
    I came to dance with the Puerto Rican women
of my class of 1967, and to remember a few pals lost in the war,
who had been so beautiful, you were happy just to look upon them,
and one more boy
lost to his own drunken wildness
under a moon who doesn't remember us.
    It's not a going back we long for, but a staying still
for one incomparable moment, all the lost loves' faces
spinning in the mirrored ball.

The Country That We Love

Before the stand that sold peaches and sweet corn in the summer,
someone had stood up a mannequin,
dressed in a gold lamé bikini and red wig
with tiny American flags in each hand that undulated in the breeze,
and I thought, isn't this the country that we love,
isn't this perspective of clouds and despair deeper than usual,
vultures circling lazily in the distance, as if at the end of a long tunnel.

At the end of the day, it rains through some sunlight. Birds gather.
They gather and swarm and make their biometric shapes against a white sky.

Elegy for Anna N.

That mad urge to pull words up my throat and out of my mouth
can be no more than a passing fancy,
     especially when it's so cold outside; even for the spirits
it's cold, but a body is floating inside of our heads
     and her lovers won't put her into the ground,

or even set her on fire. *Look what we made of her*
     are not the words of a song
although they sound that way, I know.
     If you sing your life in a certain way,
it can sound like a song of the blue and opiate water.

The Way Dante Moved Virgil Through Hell

Please, your words fly past
so quickly I am dizzy, sick,
like when clouds
zoom past so quick,
like at the carnival, remember
the dying shopping mall,
horrific in the archive of somehow,
but it was not a strange gratuity of clowns,
and had more to do with
some roughnecks who ran the rides,
but I can't remember,
so don't walk me down that
alleyway between tents,
muddy from the recent rain;
(why have they let us
out so late, and alone?).
There's scurrying,
but I don't know if it's
in my head or not;
I don't know if it's
inside of time or not;
the Tilt-a-Whirl was not my last escape,
so into the rubber night I crept,
nothing in my mind but thoughts,
then later, behind the sodden, artsy
warehouse of random longing,
behind the invasion of
certain thoughts (like having soup
later, with the girl from Binh Luc)
that have the will to lift you up
right off your feet into contrails
above the stadium

where I found some words
whispered from blowing limbs of willow
trees far away, but also alive in night sky
right above our heads as we tried
to get over the strangeness
that lingered like a thing lingers
when there's been some
hurtful problem
that sends you reeling
into thoughts of dying's
bright and faithful enterprise,
and even at the Sheetz
twenty-four-hour coffee bar,
my dying body fell in love with strangers.
Oh, the light off of that lake is so inviting
that I think of this as the end of my life,
as in the phrase
"the end of his life,"
and it could happen to you
that some cool air
blows through the window
extravagantly open to the
unattended night,
so you're delivered,
rapture style,
to another place. It
happens (to me) all the time.

PART II

My Waiting Brain

My Waiting Brain

i

There are pathways he must follow when he goes into my brain,
or else something catastrophic might happen. He said
any kind of bleeding in the brain is not good.
I think he was talking to himself. Meantime, my waiting brain said,
Love yourself; love your pain and your illnesses
waiting down the road for you like old friends in the shade. Better
spend some time tonight, looking at the stars.

ii

Empty again as the dead hawk's heart is empty of blood on the highway
        where it must have slammed into the truck's windshield at say
sixty-five miles an hour
        is how my brain says the world looks today,
although it may be this unseasonably warm winter of green grass and geese
        who don't know which way to hoot
that has my head spinning;
        the way a too warm December evening
can hold still its last moment of light, right before your eyes.

iii

Help, my waiting brain says, and then, *Fuck you.*
        He woke me up at 4 A.M.
with his pal, Mr. Spinning Room,
               in our private field of opiates,
so all I could do was lie there and listen to rain murmur in the night,
        the sound like someone who is lost,
talking to herself in the dark.

iv

Good morning highly polished chrome nightmare tool.
You look fine this morning, like a silver snake
bristling alive in every scale,
longing to be inserted into my waiting brain
to wind down the tunnels of me, once and for all.

v

      We were celebrating the birth of Jesus Christ the Savior,
by stuffing our bodies with food and wine,
so, like the Romans,
we fell into a stupor afterward,
a semi-comatose state, especially the men.
      Everyone was otherwise preoccupied,
and although I was surrounded
by the snoozing, snoring bodies of my people,
it was as if I were alone,
just my waiting brain and me. Night came
with its enormous rotation of stars,
      so something seemed possible, even if it wasn't hope,
even if the thing we spend our lives moving toward
is unknowable, until it's too late to turn back.

vi

In the dark I wanted peace,
my waiting brain told me,
as if that's too much to ask,
as if sacrifice is too much to ask,
given everything I've done for you,
and how could I argue.

vii

In the end, my waiting brain said,
 Dismantle me but don't undress,
the blue spruce watch us through the blowing snow;
forgive my forgetfulness,
but I don't remember my name.

Meditation After Prayer

Blues for Que Mai

At a bar on Hoan Kiem Lake in Hanoi,
second floor of five I think, dusky evening
settling into night with my friend,
who survived the slaughter, by Americans,
of four hundred and ninety
out of five hundred of his own. Survived
I say too easily for his sake, and he is beautifully
wild in the space around us,
around him, with his stories,
brilliant, but lost too, so deeply
he can't help but give it all away
in his eyes, the other side of the mirror,
and though we tried to toast the old pain away
with good whiskey and beer from Hanoi,
and with the fried inner organs of
animals, the haunting world would not

leave his eyes, so I wanted to hide or
to scream something out, to release the
pressure that had grown around me, and then
an angel came into the room and in
Vietnamese she sat down with us and calmed
some troubled waters. In my mind I took
her hand and walked across the room to the
empty black piano and played a streak of
B-flat blues for her, to try and escape
the velocity of my friend's hurt, if
only for a minute, and like a
river the notes flowed from my fingers,
the room trembling now around a frozen
center, until the scale runs out,

and the roaring dark
comes back into being.

For Bao Ninh

On the Little Juniata River

     The river makes a sound at night
that you almost don't want to hear:
         nearly imperceptible lap of current

that drifts upward into heavy branches
         and then up farther into night sky.
It may take you with it

         if you're not careful
and you call to spirits
         even accidentally. *This is where I've been,*

the river says at night,
         and makes a blue picture in moonlight
on its surface, of what's waiting, then is gone.

The Abundance of Nothing

It isn't nice to watch the baby sparrow
die beneath the eave's spout where it fell,
    its nest torn by a storm so black and quick.
What do you do, what do you do,
    with a life so small, small as gasps of air
the paper-thin beak tries to take in, the eyes still closed.

    (I don't want anyone
to end my misery
    unless I say so,
and you can put that in writing.)
    This time, I know how not to kill the sparrow,
but let it have the life that it has left,
    a cool wind blowing across both us, all of us,
black clouds gathering for nighttime and some rain.

What the Matter Was

Just give me a break, the guy who begs on my street corner
says every time I walk past him on my way to work.
I know you got money, he says. *I know where you live.*
He doesn't mean to threaten—although he does know
where I live—it's just that he's tried everything
to make an honest day's wages, and nothing else has worked.
I used to give him all of my loose change—it must
have been a couple hundred bucks in all—because
of the DISABLED VET sign he wore around his neck.
Brother vet, I thought, until one day I saw him
playing squash with a woman whose hair was dyed red
at a fancy club downtown where you can watch people
exercise through plate glass windows if you want to.
Afterward, they went and had coffee. I followed them.
He wasn't disabled. Seeing the way he had moved,
he was too young to have been in any war. *It's
a living,* he said, when I saw him the next day,
and knew that he knew that I knew. *Give me a break.
I know you got money. I know where you live.*

Paradise of Pain

We pray for the pain to stop out of habit,
      because we're taught to be that way, you see,

but after I left the paradise of pain,
      I was lonely, as for a lover.

What pain knows about me,
      I wouldn't tell anyone else.

For Penelope

Gypsies read in his palm that they would be
together after all of the histories,
all of the journeys inward and out. We
put our faith in beliefs that give us pleasure.
He put his faith in the gypsy who foretold
Penelope's black hair and olive skin
as if from a vision, her eyes closed tight,
her hands enfolding his hands. We believe
in what we need to believe to stay calm
or sane inside the matrix of a life
not of our choosing or design, but
irreversible as a promise made
under ancient skies. Her promise,
for example, that she made with her eyes
to him, and with her mouth, and with the flower
of her hands held before her, and with her
white thighs that she parted for him, so
in his mind he is dying of weariness,
dying of burdens in the vacuum of without her.

When I'm Gone

When I'm gone, I won't be here anymore, if you can imagine that. I can.
I can imagine being gone, and then being somewhere else, somewhere
entirely different from this place, but with mist as at Dak To,
only with softer greens and blues, and no small arms fire chatter
in the untroubled trees, and no poison-tipped bamboo sticks.

And when I'm gone, I would bequeath the space I had occupied
to the dreamers, and to the disenfranchised, and to the lost singers of songs,
so they might pitch their trash bag tents in peace
and ease back into the darkness that I love, when I'm gone.

The World, Part I

I think I'll put my pencil down
        so I can walk all through these slender winter shadows
dark green and taut as wire,
        stretched across the neighbors' lawns.

I think I'll find some peace there
        in the way they linger
just long enough these winter days
        to satisfy my desire,
and allow me to believe in something good,
        although our tragedies are so precise,
so impossible in their dying beauty to escape.

        I don't know where I would go,
except to the river, where the spirits gather too.

The river may run through your heart—you can feel it there—
        or the river may sweep away from you in the dark,
and never let you have it again.

But even the empire of the river crumbles these days.
        The only antidote is words, and the words are smothered
by a cloth stuffed into the mouths of our brothers and our sisters
        of the ancient tongue. Like you,
I see them behind my eyes;
        in the darkened doorways nearby where children sleep,
we see them.

This Boy

This president. This murder factory. This bombing protocol.

This stunning ignorance. This howl of hostages under moonlight
in the garden of the sublime betrayers of our faith. This hot wind.

This pedagogy of hate and indifference to the suffering lives,
bodies piling up in secret numbers in the desert gloom no-man's-land.

This subterfuge. This ancient history all over again. This death, this day.

This long-reaching pain back to home and the blunted, forsaken family.

This boy full of promise and stupid glory. This town. This boy. This boy.

Elegy for Liam

Insert rain into this picture
so you can feel the full weight of the words;
             insert late summer evening,
that particular failing light, *so heartbreaking* you would have said.

The neighborhood grass is green for this late in summer;
so much rain we never saw before. Insert the river
             that runs in the direction of nowhere, where time is,
and where we stood on a rock inside the water's hushed words.

How can I say this? Everything is dying around us,
and everyone, including some at the ends of pistols
             held by their own hands. What the hell
happened to staying around?

What Are You Going to Do

So then you arrive at nowhere to go
      except back to the luxurious dark, the dyed ermine on flesh
dark, and darkly you are there, among dark things,
      like trees, or other bodies
called like you from the lit windows of sleeplessness,
      and then
what are you going to do when you get there,
      say something to the darkness?

Gate

i

I'd seen a hawk against a white winter
sky, circling squirrel tracks stitched back and forth
across the snow; only in the body
can you find the spirit, there's the rub.

ii

It will be all of one thing, or all
of another. The question is, do you
vary your route or not, your centrifuge
of minor ventures into the pink?

iii

(There's heart in it, after all.) I saw the
hawk again flash low through bare snow-dusted
trees. It must be a god, it's so cold.

Letter to L.

I'm quite a bit more of a wreck than last you saw me,
and in case you haven't heard,
the matter is one of the brain,
and not the heart, but, dear friend,
I think of you those times the holes of loss open up
all around me, the loneliness like a pit I fall into,
a thought that won't let me breathe
and makes me wonder how I lost you
so easily to someone else's lie. I have been here all along,
and I've even had a catch or two with you in my mind.
I could feel the ball smack the leather. I could see
the sweet kinesiology of your release, and other things
involving rowdiness of a level better left unmentioned here, but
remembered in the halls of heaven for the grace of its stupidity.
But people let go is what happens. People give up.
There are things that I would never believe about you,
no matter what, no matter who said them, or why. I only wanted the same.

Beginning

I heard a voice in my head,
standing in the middle of a hurricane
of leaves I was trying to rake into a pile
to please my young father into seeing
that I could work like him. He laughed;
he picked me up, rake and all,
and whisked me away
into the warm coal furnace room of our family.
    The voice stayed there that night and said,
You don't belong here, and I thought
strange that of all the people in the neighborhood,
or in the city, or of all of the people in the world,
this voice would have chosen me to speak to.
    Belong where? I remember wondering.
I was where I was, and how could I be anywhere else?
But I wanted to say great things then,
as if something had washed over me;
I felt like I could stand up among my people,
and tell them the last story that they would ever need to hear.

Wrong

In the sea of wrong, and no way out, at three or four, I lied the lie of omission
when a crazy woman who lived in our apartment building
confused my voice she listened to through the wall with a water glass
with my sister's, about whom she had imagined things we never understood:
wild inexplicable deeds of a psychological nature, unheard of in those days.
One thing led to another, until she pounded the door with her fists;
her door, or our door, or both, it doesn't matter now, and then with some
toy wooden bowling pins, so that my mother called my father home from work,
a thing I had never seen happen before in my life, so a gloom hung over
everything; I was just learning to tie my shoes, and asked my father to watch
but he pushed me aside, and at the back of the porch he spoke to the crazy
woman who had beat on the doors with her fists. He listened to her story quietly
until her voice began to rise. I heard my sister's name called out in wild
condemnation for words that I had said, and still, in the wrong, I shuffled my
feet in silence and looked up at some strange and miserable clouds
blow in from the lake, changing everything.

She Said, "But It Was Only a Small Hurt"

In line at the drinking fountain desert heat bus-stop years
of complete blackness you bring back with you, circa 1968,
that took me through several states, some of which I would have to ask
kind strangers to name so I would know where I was. But
that's no big deal. No one would medicate us in those days,
so we medicated ourselves, but
　　　　back to the woman standing in line at the only drinking fountain
at the desert bus stop of veritable vultures, crying and talking
to her friend who also stood in line, and who consoled her
as friends are meant to do, her arms draped over her shoulders,
saying sweet, quiet things into her ear, and then all down her neck and breasts.

The Deer Cave Drawing in Southern China That the Chinese Girl Drew on the Napkin to Show Me Exactly Where the Character Now Used for the Word Deer Came From

Her black hair hung across her face at the angle of repose, a midnight sheen, and then I'm on the river of her eyes; have you ever seen that? Dear god.

I have been so near beauty, I will never be the same.

A Little Place on the Beach

And now the blast of spring
you have to suffer in all its exaltation;

open certain doors and you'd better know more than you do,
or the caring and the compassion becomes

something that you can't shake off,
like a chemical pain in the blood,

or like the pain of some memories that won't let go,
persistent as vultures

circling in the deepening sky,
in the measureless sky full of holes.

I don't know what comes
when the shadows

harden into walls that make a maze,
and the day's flinching light

gives way to hallucination and wonder,
but it's like a certain trouble

deep in my brain, an out-of-whack that's hard to fix,
as heartache is hard to fix inside someone.

Some dead follow you forever,
as in a boat along the shoreline

between the dazzling world
in all its neon nothing

and the body you must carry
      through the dark jungle rain,

and all I want is a little refuge,
      a little place on the beach in my mind.

Response to "Why Don't You Write About Something Happy?"

The bad fuse in the bomb that won't go off.
The drowning baby's lungs that fill with air.
The hammer fist pulled back before it strikes.
The poison coffee rendered down the drain.
The robin's nest not torn to shreds this time.
The childhood not marred by people's hands.
The gills not torn up through the fish's mouth.
The brakes that held around the dead man's curve.
The flooded street the mom and dad survive.
The razor in the locker left alone.
The hiding woman safe at last this once
from all the woes and blows she's had to bear.
The mourning cloak you didn't have to wear.

To No Spirits Speak

I wanted to break through you know and get fresh with the other side
because I kept seeing those lost ones moving back and forth mainly in the trees
you know that other world seems so close

as on the other side of the leaves the wind from nowhere turns over
dark to light but hurt can reach across those borders too
someone can call back to you through the waves of pain
and you can hear it like a loud bird trapped inside your head

South Lorain Suite

i

On my way to school I stopped at Fatty's
        Bar and Grille and watched the
policemen place their bets, so

blue their uniforms, that
        I was drunk with happiness
to be with them. Shot and

a beer I learned there, shot
        and a beer, and the drowsy
numbness of summer

afternoons, lost to vague
        desires. Those men were
our fathers, but not in

heaven; they lined the bars
        when the shift was done and
drank their paychecks to

smithereens. I remember
        the mother's voice like a
candle in the pitch night,

flickering, calling him
        home from the street to supper
and the doorway of our long shadows.

ii

Rock me awake
        the trains in the roundhouse,
the voices of trainmen

cutting through night sky
        like birds to my open
window. Everything waited

to be known beyond the
        walls of our lonely
apartment, and I had

to hold on to keep from
        spinning off the world
and be sucked into blue-

black space. There once was a
        time when kind giants ruled
the world, and protected

you, and came home. I
        don't know how to say that
I lived in the twilight

where dark wings
beat my sky to death.

The Father in Me

Flowers call to me and the blossoming
      trees call to me especially the fruit
trees the apple and cherry and pear call
      to me and the young spruce calls to me and
the lovesick dove mistakes my moans for a
      kindred spirit and calls to me but I
can't hear because the unappreciated
      raking of clawed feet across one's face to
avoid an ambush of vultures returning
      to the city by the lake fed by a
burning river or else face not the reckoning
      you might imagine. Children call to me,
mostly for money.

Apocryphal Weather

Chaos in the distant thunder I hear
    like misdirected artillery
and the ghosts
    left in its wake

and the most lovely summer
    lawn mower noise next door somewhere.
It fades, and then gets loud, and then fades again
    as long as I will listen.

Today, I won't die
    of loneliness
because the lilac scent
    blows through the screen
restoring me.

Roses for the Reader

I want to give you these roses still cool from the florist.
I want to give you these roses, dying of their own beauty.
I want you to watch them die; that's the point.
This isn't story hour with Miss Nice Pants, after all.
I want to stop lying. I want to give you these roses
I stole from the grave of someone
I did not love enough. Like the rest of us
they began to die the moment they were plucked from the earth.
Another lie is that I want you to watch them die.
I want you to crush them into your face
because that's what you do with roses
dying of our tenderness. Roses, crushed all over your face.

The Future

In the future they won't know me or see my smiling face
so they'll have only the words to go by. I wish
I could have done better.
They might want to look down into the tunnel of our skulls
to see if some light shone there once,

or they might want to shake those bones
and toss them into a dusty circle
where they might say something
about who we were and
what we were unafraid to imagine.

So to the future people
I send my best regards and my gratitude
for having taken over
just when I know
things were getting very difficult:

all the poison gas wars claptrap
and the catastrophic ignorance of men
risen from the throne of their lies.
I wish I knew less about our history of killing,
so I could see you peaceful in my mind.

Flash

And with the tanned and lovely sergeant
I watched the upper half of a peasant man
convulse in the dust,
      the lower half blown away by a two-hundred-and-fifty-pound
American bomb the Vietcong had rigged into a booby trap.
The concussion rattled my teeth and my brain.
I couldn't stop watching. For a long time, no one moved.
I couldn't lift my foot to take a single step. I was flushed,
      soaked with sweat, swooning in the movements of the dying man.
I thought that if I died too, somehow, I would be released
from the waves of sickness that rolled over me, but the sergeant
saw something like a pale curtain come over my face:
      already my eyes rolling back in my head and my knees giving way
to the stinking power of someone else's death, right before your eyes,
so he grabbed my arm and shook me
back to where I needed to be to go on. "It don't mean a thing," he said,
and we turned back to the trees, and their safe shadows, and cool.

Meditation After Prayer

It's only rain and sleet and freezing sheen over everything
that makes it all look real. The dying time so things can be born again.
Someone scratched some marks into the walls of a cave
as if to say something, as if to show the way into a world that didn't exist yet
but could be heard, like a great army, trudging across the hills from far away.
I am far away sometimes, although not entirely by choice. What happens
after prayer is a question in the form of heat that tingles my spine
just to the edge of pain, where I like it. I can't say it any other way.